More Praise for *Hello Stay Interviews, Goodbye Talent Loss*

"No one knows more about retention and motivation of top talent than Beverly Kaye and Sharon Jordan-Evans—and no one gives better advice on how to retain your high performers. Brief, to the point, and packed full of practical tips, *Hello Stay Interviews, Goodbye Talent Loss* is a sparkling gem of a book. I highly recommend it."
—**Jim Kouzes, coauthor of *The Leadership Challenge***

"Sometimes simpler is better. To win the war for talent, Bev and Sharon have developed an amazingly simple, powerful, and useful idea: the stay interview. By doing stay interviews, managers learn what employees want, help employees feel better about themselves, and increase retention of the organization's most valuable assets."
—**Dave Ulrich, Rensis Likert Professor of Business Administration, University of Michigan, and Partner, The RBL Group**

"All seasoned managers have experienced the nightmare: you're up to your eyebrows in work and suddenly your star performer hands in a resignation. Could you have done anything sooner to avoid this? The answer is a resounding *yes!* Adding Kaye and Jordan-Evans's stay interview to your management playbook will create a much happier and more productive workplace for everyone!"
—**Marshall Goldsmith, author of *What Got You Here Won't Get You There***

"This book is brilliant. If you plan on increasing your level of engagement or improving your existing performance management processes, or want to know how to keep your best employees, this is the perfect book for you."
—**Louis Carter, founder and CEO, Best Practice Institute and Skillrater**

"It's imperative that managers at all levels have effective tools to retain the best talent in an increasingly competitive marketplace. *Hello Stay Interviews, Goodbye Talent Loss* is just such a tool! It provides proven strategies that will guide leaders to take the most effective steps to keep and engage their stars!"
—**Mark Ferrara, Vice President, Talent Management, Eli Lilly and Company**

"A much needed and required book for growing organizations worldwide."
—**Rajeev Agarwal, CEO, MAQ Software**

"Having both conducted and been the recipient of stay interviews, I can attest that they work. This is a great book for any leader, no matter what size the team."
—**Troy Hayes, PsyD, Director of Talent, Leadership, and Organization Development, Ingersoll Rand**

"Beverly Kaye and Sharon Jordan-Evans have yet again provided managers a practical, valuable, easy read with great insights. *Hello Stay Interviews, Goodbye Talent Loss* truly is a manager's playbook on how to have short, effective, ongoing conversations with employees that result in their feeling valued and productive. Stay interviews are something we all should be doing as leaders!"

—Don Kraft, Head of Career and Learning, Genentech, Inc.

"Bev and Sharon provide a practical approach to help you prepare for and get the most out of these critical conversations. Read this book and you will increase your leadership effectiveness and maximize the engagement of those you lead."

—Tim Tobin, Vice President, Global Leadership Development, Marriott International, and author of *Your Leadership Story*

"The war for talent is raging around the globe. So when you land A-players, it is critical you keep them. Beverly and Sharon's stay interview is precisely the practical solution a leader needs to significantly up the odds of retaining key people."

—Verne Harnish, CEO, Gazelles, and author of *Scaling Up*

"*Hello Stay Interviews, Goodbye Talent Loss* provides an easy-to-follow playbook that any manager can apply to get those important conversations underway. Stay interviews help managers achieve healthy relationships with their employees and retain their 'keepers.'"

—Michelle Prince, Senior Vice President, Talent Management, Randstad North America

"The simple and practical tools in this book, applied regularly, will engender greater trust in you as a leader and improve the performance of your unit tenfold. Bev and Sharon have taken away any excuse you might have for *not* conducting a powerful and effective stay interview."

—Tina Sung, Vice President, Government Transformation and Agency Partnerships, Partnership for Public Service

HELLO
STAY INTERVIEWS

GOODBYE
TALENT LOSS

A MANAGER'S PLAYBOOK

Other Books by the Authors

Love 'Em or Lose 'Em: Getting Good People to Stay
Love It, Don't Leave It: 26 Ways to Get What You Want at Work

HELLO
STAY INTERVIEWS

GOODBYE
TALENT LOSS

A MANAGER'S PLAYBOOK

BEVERLY KAYE AND
SHARON JORDAN-EVANS

Coauthors of the international bestseller *Love 'Em or Lose 'Em*

$\overline{\text{BK}}$®

Berrett–Koehler Publishers, Inc
a BK Business book

Berrett-Koehler Publishers, Inc.
1333 Broadway, Suite 1000
Oakland, CA 94612-1921
Tel: (510) 817-2277
Fax: (510) 817-2278
www.bkconnection.com

Ordering Information

Quantity sales. Special discounts are available on quantity purchases by corporations, associations, and others. For details, contact the "Special Sales Department" at the Berrett-Koehler address above.

Individual sales. Berrett-Koehler publications are available through most bookstores. They can also be ordered directly from Berrett-Koehler: Tel: (800) 929-2929; Fax: (802) 864-7626; www.bkconnection.com

Orders for college textbook/course adoption use. Please contact Berrett-Koehler: Tel: (800) 929-2929; Fax: (802) 864-7626.

Orders by U.S. trade bookstores and wholesalers. Please contact Ingram Publisher Services, Tel: (800) 509-4887; Fax: (800) 838-1149; E-mail: customer.service@ingrampublisherservices.com; or visit www.ingrampublisherservices.com/Ordering for details about electronic ordering.

Berrett-Koehler and the BK logo are registered trademarks of Berrett-Koehler Publishers, Inc.

Printed in the United States of America

Berrett-Koehler books are printed on long-lasting acid-free paper. When it is available, we choose paper that has been manufactured by environmentally responsible processes. These may include using trees grown in sustainable forests, incorporating recycled paper, minimizing chlorine in bleaching, or recycling the energy produced at the paper mill.

Library of Congress Cataloging-in-Publication Data
Kaye, Beverly L.
Hello stay interviews, goodbye talent loss : a manager's playbook /
Beverly Kaye and Sharon Jordan-Evans. — First edition.
        pages cm
Includes bibliographical references.
        ISBN 978-1-62656-347-6 (pbk.)
        1. Employee retention. 2. Employment interviewing. 3. Personnel
        management. I. Jordan-Evans, Sharon, 1946- II. Title.
HF5549.5.R58K387 2014
658.3'14—dc23
                                                                2015002637

First Edition

20 19 18 17   10 9 8 7 6 5 4 3 2

Text design and composition: Seventeenth Street Studios
Cover design and illustrations: Mike Rohde
Copyeditor: Todd Manza
Proofreader: Laurie Dunn
Indexer: Richard Evans

To my kids and their kids.
Thanks for bringing such joy and
adventure to my life!
—SHARON

To my colleagues, friends, and family.
(You know who you are!)
I stay creative, confident, and connected
because of your support.
—BEV

Contents

Preface

■ We developed the idea of stay interviews in 1997, before publishing the first edition of *Love 'Em or Lose 'Em* (San Francisco: Berrett-Koehler, 1999). It came from work with an organization worried about losing a key group of talent. We suggested that they ask those people "What will keep you here?" and then use the responses to craft their retention strategies. It seemed so basic and so simple. Yet, up to that time, managers seldom asked that question in such a straightforward way. Or they asked it in an exit interview, which is almost always too late.

Managers today need leadership tools and techniques that they can deploy easily and that make sense. The stay interview is one of those tools. We've seen that managers who practiced stay interviews and then took action not only retained talent but also developed more engaged, committed, and productive teams. Some organizations have even mandated stay interviews and hold managers accountable for reporting on what they are learning.

Stay interviews have caught on. Now thousands of managers in hundreds of organizations, large and small, are using this simple, straightforward, easy-to-implement strategy. We wrote this playbook to outline the process, give hints and tips about dealing with tough requests, and share stories of managers who've been using stay interviews to keep their valued employees engaged and on their teams.

This book offers you a simple idea. It is designed for the not-so-simple task of letting talented people know that you value them, need them, and want them to remain as contributing members of your team.

BEV AND SHARON

HELLO
STAY INTERVIEWS

GOODBYE
TALENT LOSS

A MANAGER'S PLAYBOOK

stay in·ter·view*
[stey] / ˈ ɪntər, vyu/ [in-ter-vyoo]

adjective, noun

- a conversation between a manager and a valued employee

- an opportunity to learn more about an employee and to show you care

- a chance to find out what might keep an employee in the organization and or on the team

- a chat that causes employees to feel highly valued

- a process found most effective when repeated often

*as defined by *Bev and Sharon*

Invitation

W E INVITE YOU to conduct stay interviews with anyone you hope will stay engaged and on your team.

When do most managers ask "What can I do to keep you?" You guessed it: during exit interviews. It's a great question, but the timing is off. We suggest you ask it sooner.

You want them to stay—at least for a while longer. They are your stars and your highfliers. And they are your solid citizens too—the people who show up every day to do the work you need them to do. Your competition wants them, and you can't afford to lose them.

Help Them Say Why They Stay

■ You don't have to cling desperately to your talent. You can keep them pumped up and excited about coming to work for you every day. Find out what will keep them engaged and on your team.

If you're not yet holding stay interviews, you are guessing at what your talented people really want—from you, from the team, from their work. You could be guessing wrong. Stay interviews are just one of many strategies in a successful manager's playbook. But they are absolutely foundational to engaging, motivating, recognizing, and retaining talent.

3

It seems so simple—just *ask!* Yet most managers will admit they are not conducting stay interviews (and their bosses are not conducting them, either). Why? Often it's because they're afraid of the answers.

They ask, "What if I ask my talented people what will keep them and they all say money or a promotion?" Good point. So the fear of being unable to deliver on someone's request gets in the way of having the most crucial dialogue of all. Is that true for you? This book offers you an easy four-step process you can use when an employee tosses you a tough-to-deliver-on request. It works like magic.

If you manage even one person, we're betting you've conducted at least one stay interview. You probably didn't call it that or think of it exactly in those terms. But your intention was no doubt twofold:

1. to let your talented employee know how much you value him, and

2. to find out what will keep her engaged and on your team.

That's a stay interview! It's not complex. It's simply talking to your employees about what matters most and then working together to make that happen.

You might wonder, *If it's that simple, why would you write a whole book about it?* Good question. The short answer is: because managers asked us for it. Many leaders first learned about the concept in our book *Love 'Em or Lose 'Em: Getting Good People to*

Stay. For several years they've asked us to dive in to this topic to help them:

- ▸ better understand how stay interviews really work;

- ▸ quickly and easily prepare for these important conversations;

- ▸ effectively deal with tough requests coming their way;

- ▸ have these conversations in different cultures; and

- ▸ really *enjoy* these ongoing dialogues with the talented people on their teams.

We purposefully designed this to be a playbook. We wanted it to be user friendly, a quick reference tool, and something you'll turn to often. We designed it for managers with heavy schedules and ongoing pressure to deliver results. It's also useful to recruiters—the professionals with whom managers partner to seek talent and then to screen, interview, and select a match that will last.

We invite you to take the time to conduct stay interviews and to take action on what you learn. Conduct these conversations early and often, with everyone you hope will bring their best and stick around for a while. Your return on investment will be an increased understanding of those on your team. And what might that lead to? Increased commitment, productivity, innovation, and success for you, your team, and the organization.

WHY BOTHER?

CHAPTER ONE

Why Bother?

■ Why bother? What's in it for you?

You're busy, perhaps busier than you've ever been in your life. Why would you consider adding one more item to your overwhelming to-do list? Why take the time and make the effort to conduct stay interviews?

The answer is that you should conduct stay interviews because you want to:

- ▶ **better understand all of your employees.** What makes them unique and special? What do they bring to the team? And what do they want more of . . . or less of?

- ▶ **demonstrate that you value them as human beings, that you care.** This assumes, of course, you actually do care.

- ▶ **encourage them to stay on your team.** It's very expensive to lose them. You want them to stay, both physically and psychologically. You want them to love coming to work with you and for you. You want them to bring their creativity, energy, and effort with them.

The Cost of Loss

■ You've already seen the numbers. You know, the ones that tell you
how much it costs when a talented employee walks out your door.
It's been well documented that it costs 70 percent to 400 percent
of an employee's annual salary to replace him or her. Some of
those costs are easy to measure and are sometimes called "hard
costs." Think about one talented person you lost recently. What
did it cost your organization to replace her? Did you:

> ▶ recruit on job boards or run Internet ads?

> ▶ hire a headhunter?

> ▶ pay a referral fee?

> ▶ cover candidates' interview expenses, such as airlines,
> hotels, meals, or cabs?

> ▶ commit to a larger salary or give a sign-on bonus to the
> new recruit?

> ▶ offer a moving allowance?

> It adds up.

Soft Costs Are Costlier

■ Then there are the harder-to-measure soft costs. These represent
the more subtle effects and costs of talent lost. Which of these have
you seen? And what did it *really* cost you and your organization?

You'll lose time interviewing.

If you weren't interviewing all those candidates for the job your terrific employee left, what would you be doing instead? You'd be building, selling, designing, leading, brainstorming, connecting, teaching . . . and more. We rest our case.

Productivity plummets during a job search.

You start losing money the moment your talented employees disengage. Instead of working for you, they're updating their résumés, logging on to job boards and social media, responding to potential employers, interviewing, negotiating, accepting the new job—and then celebrating. Their departure is a pricey proposition.

When someone leaves, the work doesn't.

Work doesn't go away just because the person handling it leaves. It simply gets put on hold or redistributed until a replacement is found. And very often that replacement never materializes. The image of a hamster on a treadmill is all too accurate. The result is burnout and lower morale for all those who've stayed.

When one goes, others follow.

Talented people find greener grass and then call their buddies, enticing them to follow. This happens even more often today, particularly among younger workers, who highly value both flexibility and friendships.

They'll take their brilliance and (perhaps) your customers with them.

Have you ever had a loyal customer follow you to your next job? What did that cost the organization you left? And what about the brilliance and the institutional knowledge that wanders out the door with that person you cannot afford to lose? Tally that.

No one enters fully ready.

How long does it take to teach new employees the ropes? How long before they know how to navigate your organization, talk to your customers, integrate with other business units, or move an idea? Meanwhile, the team carries the load . . . at what cost?

New hires don't always measure up.

It's a risk you take when you're replacing a great employee. If the new hire isn't as productive, personable, or knowledgeable as the one you lost, what is the cost?

Run the numbers

There's only so much you can do without the people you need to get the job done. There's only so far you can reach, only so many fires you can put out, and only so many projects you can take on. The next time you wonder whether stay interviews are worth your time and effort, run the numbers. Calculate both the hard and the soft costs of talent loss. Then call your employees in and find out what will keep them engaged and on your team. Do you wonder how to do that? Read on.

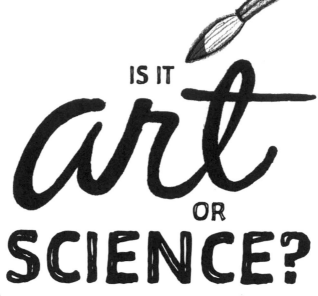

IS IT
art
OR
SCIENCE?

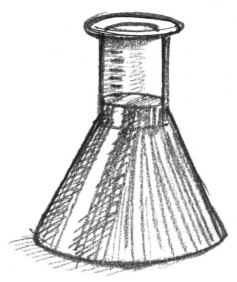

CHAPTER TWO

Is It Art or Science?

■ Is the stay interview an art or a science? It's both.

The best stay interviews are a perfect blend of two things:

1. **The person you bring to it.** That's about your authenticity, attitude, and mind-set.

2. **The process, tools, and action steps you use.** We're giving you some of those in this book.

Great stay interviews require your genuine caring and curiosity. They also involve creating just the right questions, given your style and the employee's. They require anticipating what your talented employees might ask of you and carefully preparing for any hard-to-deliver-on requests. And they include listening artfully as people tell you what matters most to them.

A Stay Interview by Any Other Name

■ You might be thinking that this sounds like the once-a-year conversations you're required to have with your employees. But is it really? Or is that annual (often mandatory) conversation actually a performance appraisal? You know, where you list what they've done well, where they've fallen short, and what you hope they'll do differently next year.

Or perhaps it's an individual development planning discussion. These conversations focus on what your employees want to learn next.

Or maybe it's a career discussion? Chats about careers are often about employees' career goals. It's a discussion about next steps.

The stay interview might include components of every one of these types of conversations. When you ask a question like "What will keep you here?," the answer might prompt a discussion about career, performance, or learning opportunities. But the dialogue often goes well beyond those topics. It could include discussions of work/life balance concerns, or how to manage conflict with a teammate, or what your employees really want and need from you.

> *"What will keep you here? What might entice you away?"* These are the most powerful stay interview questions, the granddaddies of them all. Until you try them, you won't believe the positive impact they can have on the talented people you hope to keep on your team. And you'll be amazed at the new information you'll receive.

Beyond those questions, there are dozens of other terrific queries you can use, depending on variables such as your relationship with this person, the organization's culture, the situation at hand, your goals for the conversation, your comfort level, and your experience with stay interviews.

Some of Our Favorites

■ Here are a few of our favorite questions and the reasons why we like them.

"What about your job makes you jump out of bed in the morning?" This question conjures up an image immediately and gets your employee thinking about why he's excited about going to work. It is an unexpected question about job satisfaction, and it typically elicits some fascinating responses, such as "The project I'm working on" or "Seeing my favorite client" or "Handling a tough problem" or "I love my colleagues." You will learn more about your employee just by asking this question.

"What makes you hit the snooze button?" What a safe way to ask someone what she does not like as much about her job! Employees have answered this question in diverse and informative ways, such as "I'm just not an early-morning person." Perhaps you could flex just a bit regarding her start time, or allow her to catch up on e-mails from home and then hit the freeway after rush hour. Another talented employee said he dreaded Monday morning staff meetings and delayed his trek to work for as long as possible. Could that staff meeting be shorter, better planned, or moved to another time?

"If you were to win the lottery and resign, what would you miss the most about your job?" Who doesn't dream about winning the lottery? Yet most of us, truth be told,

would miss something about our job if we were to leave. Many employees will answer, "I'd miss the people most." Yet others stay on the job *despite* the people! Think how valuable it is to know who wants what.

"What do you want to learn this year?" He could answer, "Nothing. Nope, don't want to learn anything this year." (Hope you don't have more than one of these folks on your team.) The question elicits fascinating responses that can help you gauge employees' desire to learn, in general, and also can surface ideas for enriching their jobs.

"Does work give you back as much as it takes out of you?" Wow—now there's a powerful question! What's *your* answer to it? And what would we learn about you based on that answer?

Manager favorites

▶ *"If you had a magic wand, what would be the one thing you would change about this department/team/organization?"*

▶ *"As your manager, what could I do a little more of or a little less of?"*

▶ *"What can we do to support your career goals?"*

▶ *"How important is your work to you? Why?"*

▶ *"What makes for a great day?"*

▶ *"Do you get enough recognition? How do you like to be recognized?"*

▶ *"'I love it!' When was the last time you said this about your job? This morning? Last week? You can't remember when?"*

▸ *"What do you wish you had known before you took this job?"*

▸ *"What has been a pleasant surprise?"*

▸ *"If you had a friend coming to work here, what would you tell him?"*

One manager asks, "What's your favorite candy?" Then he has that candy on hand for times when he wants to show appreciation for a job well done. How's that for an engagement tactic?

Conversation Catalysts

■ Some of you are now ready to have stay interviews with your talented people. Others have asked us to share some sentence starters to kick-start these conversations. We've categorized these according to what your goals for the stay interview might be and what you hope to learn about your talented employee.

Empower the employee.

▸ *"I'd like to know what you would like to talk about . . ."*

▸ *"Let's plan our time together . . ."*

▸ *"I hope you'll feel free to initiate these chats in the future . . ."*

Double-check what you know.

▸ *"From our past conversations, it would appear . . ."*

▸ *"It seems you really like to . . ."*

▸ *"Last time we talked, you mentioned . . ."*

Find out something entirely new.

- ▶ *"It would help me to understand better . . ."*
- ▶ *"We've never talked about your . . ."*
- ▶ *"You know, I really don't know how you . . ."*
- ▶ *"Have you ever thought about . . ."*

Inquire about putting an action in motion.

- ▶ *"If you could do X, would that cause you to . . ."*
- ▶ *"What if you were to . . ."*
- ▶ *"What if I could . . ."*
- ▶ *"What if you could . . ."*
- ▶ *"What if nothing changed around . . ."*

Learn about an attitude or feeling.

- ▶ *"So how do you feel about . . ."*
- ▶ *"How would you feel if you took on . . ."*
- ▶ *"Would things change for you if . . ."*

Confirm whether an idea might work.

- ▶ *"So if I were to do . . . you would . . ."*
- ▶ *"So if we could do . . . that would increase your . . ."*
- ▶ *"So let me recap: we're saying that . . ."*
- ▶ *"Are you committed to . . ."*

Questions are important. Listening to the answers is even more important. Beyond listening, your response (both verbal and nonverbal) is crucial. Answers such as "That's unrealistic" or "Tell me why you are worth that" will halt the dialogue and cause employees to clam up—maybe permanently. Instead, tell the truth about the barriers to saying yes, and at the same time demonstrate that you care enough to get creative and to go the extra mile for your talent. Then dive deeply to find solutions that work for you, for them, and for the organization.

Follow the Blinking Word

■ Are you often praised for being a terrific listener? If so, skip this section. But if not, read on.

Everyone agrees that active listening is foundational to effective management. That's why building that skill is core to every good leadership development program. Yet managers continually struggle with it. Some have simply not practiced it enough or had honest feedback about how often and how effectively they listen. Others let their fast-paced workdays squeeze out listening time. They rely on assumptions and quickly push to conclusions. They might save time, but they often miss the message or the meaning behind the message.

We have a recommendation. We suggest that you *follow the blinking word*. As your talented employees answer your questions, you'll notice words that "blink." Ask questions about those words. Here's how it worked for one manager and his talented employee.

MANAGER: What's the best part of your day?

EMPLOYEE: I really like it when I get to solve a complex problem, one where I need to bring in colleagues to really get to the bottom of it.

Which words blink, or stand out? Which pique curiosity or invite more discussion? Some of you will say the words that blink in this example are *complex* or *problem* or *complex problem*. Others will hear *bring in colleagues* as the blinking words. Any of these words could work.

Notice how this manager follows the blinking word and dives in —and then watches again for the blinking words and follows one with a question.

MANAGER: Say more about your interest in solving complex problems. Not everyone enjoys that. When did that start for you?

EMPLOYEE: I guess that ever *since I was a kid* I've enjoyed it. I used to love those puzzles, like Rubik's Cube, that drive some people crazy. My friends and I would sometimes *work together* on it. Other times we'd *compete* and see who could finish first.

MANAGER: Ah—so the puzzles and competition started in your childhood. How do those experiences translate to your current job?

EMPLOYEE: Well, first of all, I have plenty of Rubik's Cubes in this job! And my *colleagues* can often help me *solve the problem*. That's great, and there's an element of *fun* for me when I'm collaborating with others.

The manager has so many possible paths to follow now. The secret is to not move to a completely different question (or topic) right away but to truly stay the course, listen for another blinking word, and dive in. Employees will feel heard and better understood in an exchange like this.

One manager asked, "What if I ask the wrong question and go down the wrong path?" Don't worry. Your employee will help you course-correct, as in this next example.

MANAGER: So, would you like to have more of your work be team-based rather than solo? If so, how much more?

EMPLOYEE: Well, not necessarily. If a problem is *pretty straightforward* I'd rather just do it and get it behind me.

I want others in the mix when the problem is complex and many heads are better than one.

MANAGER: Great. This is so helpful. Let's continue talking about which projects you'd like to team on and which you'd rather do on your own.

Notice how the manager used primarily open questions while following the blinking words. Open questions begin with words such as *how, why, where, when,* and *tell me about.* They are designed to avoid yes-or-no responses, which often lead to a dead end. As you follow the blinking word, you go deeper into your employees' situations. Meanwhile, they feel listened to. They believe that you care about their interests and goals.

The blinking word technique will encourage you to listen empathetically, at the deepest level. You will not be able to tune in and out and still follow the blinking word. (P.S. *Do* try this at home. Your spouse, kids, and friends will be pleasantly surprised at what a good listener you have become.)

The Art/Science Combo

■ Great stay interviews are a combination of art and science, questioning and listening. They're not difficult, especially if you're interested in others. Take your genuine caring and curiosity to the stay interview. Wonder about and then ask your talented employees what will keep them engaged and on your team. Listen carefully, follow the blinking words, and dive in. You'll be amazed at what you learn about the people you can least afford to lose. If this now sounds possible but you still have some reservations, read on.

What's HOLDING you BACK?

CHAPTER THREE

What's Holding You Back?

■ What's holding you back? Are you worried about what they'll ask for?

Picture this: Your boss calls you in and says, "You are so important to me and to this team. I probably don't tell you that often enough. But I can't imagine losing you. So I'd like to know, what will keep you here . . . and happy? And what might entice you away?"

Have you ever had a boss do that, perhaps in almost those exact words? If so, how did it feel? We've asked hundreds of people that question, and in response we hear things like, "It felt great. I felt important. I felt valued." One manager raised his hand and said, "It felt a little late. It was in the exit interview."

The Fear Factor

■ If it was a little late for you, or if you've never had a boss do that, you're not alone. In fact, less than 10 percent of employees have had a boss tell them how much they matter, let alone ask what will keep them engaged and on the team.

Instead, well-intentioned bosses just keep guessing. And they often guess wrong. They guess you want a promotion when you really want to learn something new. Or they guess you want a raise when you'd prefer more time off to be with your family.

Stop guessing and start conducting stay interviews with anyone you hope to keep engaged and on your team. This strategy is so simple and so foundational to all other engagement strategies. Yet managers often avoid this kind of asking. Why is that? Most often, it's the fear factor.

Afraid of What?

■ We know what you're thinking. *Why would I ask a question like that? What if my treasured, talented employee asks for something I can't give?*

> My boss told me how much he values me and asked what would keep me here. I answered honestly: a 10 percent raise would do it. He turned pale, paused, then said, "Sorry, but you're at the top of your pay scale." I was gone six months later.

So there you have it. This manager cared enough to ask, and look where it got him. He was not yet prepared for a challenging request.

Most of you aren't conducting stay interviews because you fear one of two common responses: a request for a raise or a request for a promotion. In some cultures, tough-to-deliver-on requests might also include such things as flexible work hours or location, extended leave opportunities, or job sharing. What if you can't deliver on those kinds of requests . . . at least, not right now?

The next time one of your talented employees asks for something that you might not be able to give, respond using these steps:

Four Steps for Dealing with Tough Requests

1. **Acknowledge** the request and restate how much you value them.

2. **Tell the truth about the obstacles you face in granting their requests.**

3. **Care enough to look into their requests and to stand up for them.**

4. **Ask, "What else?"** (Keep asking "what else?"—you'll eventually get something you can work with!)

It seems pretty straightforward. But how might it really play out?

He Dared to Ask

■ Antonio set up a meeting with his plant manager, Ken, for Monday morning. After some brief conversation about the weekend activities, Antonio said, "Ken, you are critical to me and to this organization. I'm not sure I've told you that directly or often enough. But you are. I can't imagine losing you. So I'd like to know what will keep you here. And what might entice you away?"

Ken was a bit taken aback—but felt flattered. He thought for a moment and then said, "You know, I aspire to move up in the organization at some point, and I'd love to have some exposure to the senior team. I'd like to see how they operate—and frankly, I'd like them to get to know me too."

Antonio responded, "I could take you with me to some senior staff meetings. Would that be a start?"

Ken said, "That would be great."

Antonio delivered on Ken's request one week later.

Well, that was easy. But what if Ken had asked for a raise? Here's how the discussion between Antonio and Ken could have gone.

Following Antonio's question about what will keep him, Ken replied immediately, "A 10 percent raise will do it!"

Now, some managers would say things like "Are you kidding?" or "Why do you think you deserve that?" Either response shuts down the dialogue and makes a key employee feel less than key. Antonio was ready for this possibility, though. Here is how he would have responded to Ken's request for a raise, using the four-step process.

1. **Acknowledge:** *You are worth that and more to me.*

2. **Tell the truth:** *I'd like to say yes, but I will need to investigate the possibility. I'm honestly not sure what I can do immediately, given some recent budget cuts.*

3. **Care enough:** *But I hear your request. I'll chat with Human Resources and my manager about it and get back to you by next Friday with answers and a possible time line for a raise.*

4. **Ask what else:** *Meanwhile, Ken, what else matters to you? What else are you hoping for?*

Research shows clearly that people want more from work than just a paycheck. When you ask the question "What else?" (possibly several times), we guarantee there will be at least one thing your talented employee wants that you can give. Remember to listen actively as your employees talk about what will keep them on your team or in your organization.

Here's another example of how one manager worked through a stay interview, using the four steps.

Mara was nervous about conducting stay interviews with her five direct reports. Her company had just weathered the recession and was hit hard. Belts were tightened, salaries were frozen, and people had been laid off. It seemed crazy to ask people what would keep them, given this scenario. Mara feared that asking would put her and her employees in a very awkward situation. But her manager said, "We're all doing it. Every manager in the company is supposed to conduct stay interviews with their talent."

So Mara prepared for the stay interview with Isaac. She decided to take him to lunch so they'd have a relaxed and private setting. Here is how the conversation went.

> **MARA:** [Notice how she acknowledges Isaac for his specific contributions.] Thank you, Isaac, for taking the time to have lunch with me. I really wanted to thank you for all you've done during our recent tough times. You've remained optimistic when others were not. You've been doing the job of two people since the layoffs and I know how hard that has been. Bottom line is, you are very important to me and to the team and organization. I want you to know that. In fact, I can't imagine losing you. So I'd like to know, what will keep you here?

ISAAC: Wow. Thanks, Mara, for saying that. I've wondered sometimes if anyone really noticed my hard work and commitment. It feels great that you did notice. To be honest, the thing that will keep me here is getting back to a more normal workload. I've already talked with my wife about this and we agreed I'd probably look for another job if that doesn't happen by the end of the year.

What can Mara do now? Watch how she uses the four steps.

MARA: [1. **Acknowledge.**] Isaac, I'm so glad we're talking. I really don't want to lose you. And I hear your need to get back to a normal workload. [2. **Tell the truth.**] What we need is another person to share the work with you, and to be honest, I'm not sure when we'll get the approval to hire that person. [3. **Care enough.**] I'll talk to Jim about this and see what we can do and by when. There must be some interim help available until we can fill that position. Let's schedule a meeting for next Friday to discuss what I've learned and what might work best for you. [4. **Ask "What else?"**] Meanwhile, what else will keep you here? For example, is there something you'd like to learn this year? Is there a longer-range goal you have in mind? Perhaps we can work together on making that happen!

ISAAC: When the workload gets back to normal, I'd like to learn to use that new software system I just heard about. Lynn has offered to mentor me, if you approve. Thanks so much for lunch and this chat, Mara. I feel more encouraged about my work situation than I have in months. It means a lot to me that you took the time to have this conversation.

Can you imagine how awkward this chat might have been had Mara not used the four steps to deal with a potentially challenging request?

Some of you are thinking, *What if the answer to "What else?" continues to be "Nothing else"?* The only thing Isaac wants is to get back to a normal workload . . . and soon!

Be honest. Acknowledge the challenge you face in making this happen and remind him you'll talk with Jim (your boss) soon. Meanwhile, suggest that you both think about possible options and work-arounds in support of Isaac's request. And set a date to talk again soon.

Now you're thinking, *What if, after all of this, there is no solution?*

It's true . . . sometimes you'll lose a person you really hoped would stay, because you simply couldn't give him what he wanted. But if you hadn't had the conversation you would have lost him anyway. You gave it your best shot and he knows that. The stay interview payoffs are many. In this case, the talent you lost still could become an ambassador for you and your organization. He could refer business or talent your way. He could even be a "boomerang" and come back to work with you someday.

Feel the Fear…and Do It Anyway

■ Susan Jeffers wrote a great book called *Feel the Fear… and Do It Anyway* (New York: Random House, 1987). That statement applies here. Notice what makes you uncomfortable about holding stay interviews with people. Acknowledge your fear when you feel it. Then, just do it. And if something else is stopping you, see whether we cover it in the next chapter.

WHAT ELSE IS WORRYING you?

My Worry List

☐ What if she asks _____?

☐ What if I can't _____?

☐ How can I deliver _____?

CHAPTER FOUR

What Else Is Worrying You?

■ What else is worrying you? Can't put your finger on it?

Managers' most common fear is that they will be unable to deliver on employees' requests. You now know how to successfully navigate that potentially tricky situation by using four simple steps. But managers have told us they have other worries, too, and that some of those concerns prevent them from conducting stay interviews. Check out these *what ifs*. Do any of them feel familiar?

What If You Ask What They Want and They Say, "I Don't Know"?

■ Remember that this is not an interrogation . . . it's a conversation, and hopefully one in an ongoing series of conversations. It's okay not to know. Some people will be surprised by your questions and need some time to think about it. Let them think, schedule another meeting, and set the stage for an ongoing dialogue about your employees' wants, needs, and career goals. Engaging and keeping your talent is a process, not an event.

By the way, a psychologist once told us that when you ask questions and the answer is "I don't know," you can ask, "Well, if you did know . . ." and you'll get an answer! Go figure.

What If You Fear Putting Ideas into Employees' Heads?

■ Seriously? As if they never thought about leaving on their own?

What If They Question Your Motivation?

■ Be honest. If you're not in the habit of having dialogues like these, it could feel strange—for you and perhaps for them. If they smile and ask, "What book have you just read?," tell them that yes, you did read a book or attend a course, and you did it because they matter to you. Tell them you honestly want to hear their answers and you want to partner with them to help them get what they want and need. You might even choose to admit that this approach sometimes feels awkward, even uncomfortable. That name-it-to-claim-it, forthright action can be just what's needed to build trust with the talent you hope will stay and play on your team.

What If It's Just Not Your Style to Ask?

BANKER: [From the audience] If I asked my employees questions like this, they'd fall over in a dead faint. I don't even say hi in the hallway.

US: Well—you might want to ease into this, then. Maybe start with hi in the hallway.

Indeed, some of you will want to ease into this. Start with an employee you know loves you, then move to the potentially more challenging conversations. The more you learn from your treasured employees, the more comfortable you'll be with *asking*.

What If You Actually Hope They Will Go?

MANAGER: [At a leadership conference] I have a very poor performer on my team. I'm trying to imagine telling him how important he is to me and to the team—and then asking what will keep him here. It seems disingenuous. How am I supposed to have a stay interview with him?

US: You definitely need to have a chat with him—but it's a performance chat, not a stay interview.

US: [Qualifying a bit] On the other hand, maybe he's not performing because you've never held a stay interview with him. Might he perform better in a different role, with different tasks or teammates—or with a different boss?

What If Cultural Differences Make You Nervous about Asking?

■ How do cultural differences play out in this crucial, foundational engagement strategy—the stay interview? We asked colleagues and clients around the globe, and the majority said that it works just as well in their regions as in the United States. However, asking questions isn't always encouraged, especially in more hierarchical cultures. One colleague told us that Asian employees need more "permission" to speak up, due to power differences and cultures of compliance that expect people to do what's needed and to avoid causing trouble. Managers in such cultures need to nudge employees more, ask more open-ended questions, and watch nonverbal cues during the conversation.

If you manage others in a culture where asking is not accepted or recommended, you'll need to find a work-around. Some managers have used anonymous surveys or tasked someone else with the "asking." However you seek to learn about what your talented employees really want, it is crucial that you do gain that information.

For instance, one global company hired a team of external consultants to conduct stay interviews with key employees in the organization. All interviewees had an opportunity to read the transcript of their interviews and to make additions or deletions. They then approved the final, confidential document that was given to their managers.

One of the managers said he would rather have had one-on-one conversations, but he knew it would have made some of his employees very uncomfortable. This work-around helped him to get what he needed from his multicultural work team in a safe and effective way.

What If They Are Younger (Older), Introverted (Extroverted), or Smarter than You?

■ This is about all those other differences we worry about. Stop worrying and start exploring the preferences and unique characteristics of each of your employees. Get to know them better and customize your approach to each individual. A spontaneous stay interview could work well with one person, whereas others want you to give them some warning, maybe even a list of questions to help them prepare.

What If It Really Is All about the Money?

■ If employees see compensation as noncompetitive, unfair, or simply insufficient to sustain life, their dissatisfaction levels will go up. They will become vulnerable to talent theft or will begin looking around for something better, especially in a favorable job market. But here's the rub: although inadequate pay can be a huge source of dissatisfaction, even fair pay won't retain people who are unhappy in other key areas. If your talented people do not feel challenged or developed or cared about, a big paycheck will not keep them for long. Researchers have found this to be true over time. In the 1950s Frederic Herzberg (*The Motivation to Work*, New York: Wilcy, 1959) found that pay is a "hygiene factor." Make sure it's there, or it will be noticed.

It is true that some people are motivated primarily by money. If that's the case, you might honestly have trouble hanging on to some of them. When you ask "What else?" four times, an employee might answer "Nothing else" each time. One senior leader said he'd learned that it is pointless to try to hang on to talent with money alone, because there is always a higher bidder. Pay fairly and competitively and then focus on the stay factors you *can* influence.

All That Good Worry Wasted

■ Some managers have said they lost sleep over holding stay interviews with their talented people. Then they did it; they held the conversations and everything worked out well. Their employees thanked them for taking the time and caring enough to ask key questions.

Employees report feeling valued by the mere gesture of their bosses telling them how important they are to the organization and asking what will keep them engaged and on the team. And bosses report that they can usually deliver on the requests. Their talented people asked for such things as more feedback, a chance to learn something new, a slight shift in arrival time to avoid rush hour, or an opportunity to serve on a newly formed task force.

If your employees are hesitant to answer your questions for any reason, you may need to build a more trusting relationship with them before you can expect honest, heartfelt responses. Just how to do that is the subject of the next chapter.

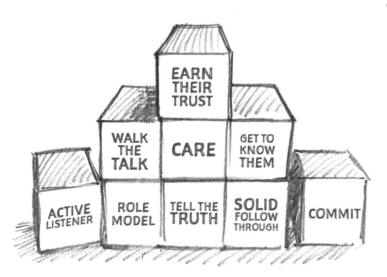

CHAPTER FIVE

Do They Trust You Enough?

■ Do they trust you enough? We hope the answer is yes.

Some people said we could skip this chapter, that everyone already knows about this. Others said that trust has nothing to do with stay interviews. Still others said that this book would be incomplete without a trust chapter. We're with them!

We've noticed that trust has everything to do with stay interviews. In fact, trust (actually lack of trust) is often the "elephant in the room." No one wants to really talk about it or recognize it, so we talk over it, under it, around it. Ultimately, though, the elephant *is* in the way, so we have to acknowledge it. And often we need to do something about it!

Trust Is the Backdrop

■ Think back to a time when you had a manager you didn't completely trust. How might a stay interview have gone? Here is what some in this situation have said:

▶ *"I consciously kept all conversations with her light, even superficial."*

▶ *"I avoided telling the truth about how I really felt or what I really wanted."*

▶ *"I never shared my career or life goals with that manager, fearing what he might do with the information."*

▶ *"I never felt fully committed to that manager or the organization."*

So what is the result for managers? They miss out. They lack pertinent information about their valued employees. And they lose out on clues for motivating, engaging, and retaining their talent. And how are employees affected? The conversation accomplishes nothing. Because they hold back, they miss an opportunity to possibly get more of what they want and need at work.

Trust is the backdrop for authentic, important conversations. Successful stay interviews happen when your talented employees trust you. They need to trust that you genuinely care about them, want to learn more about them, and have their backs—and that you'll do the right thing with information they give you in a stay interview.

If you have strong, trusting relationships with your employees, start having ongoing stay interviews now.

If you *don't* have strong, trusting relationships with your employees, start having ongoing stay interviews now. Those conversations will actually help to build trust with the people you hope to keep engaged and on your team. Paradoxical, isn't it?

How Trustworthy Are You?

■ You think you're trustworthy. But how might others view you? It depends on them, to some degree. And it depends on your actions.

How often do you behave in the following ways? Score yourself. A score of 1 means you seldom behave this way; 3 means you sometimes do and sometimes don't behave this way; and 5 means you always behave this way. (Double-check your fives with someone who knows you very well.)

TRUST-BUILDING BEHAVIORS QUIZ	Score (1 = seldom; 5 = always)
I tell the truth. I'm authentic.	
I commit and then I follow through.	
I have their backs. I'm here to catch them if they fall.	
I give clear direction and cocreate tangible goals with people.	
I lead the way. I go first sometimes, especially when there's risk.	
I keep confidences.	
I treat people with respect.	
I communicate openly.	
I show that I'm interested and that I care.	
I'm consistent in my actions. People know what to expect from me.	
I treat people fairly.	
I'm the lead cheerleader for my people.	
I walk my talk. I live my values.	
TOTAL SCORE *(out of 65)*	

How did you score? And more importantly, so what? If you gave yourself less than 65, you have at least a bit of room for improvement. Pay close attention to the trust-building behavior scores you hope to improve. Take action—start practicing those behaviors, and watch the reaction from the people you hope to engage and retain.

For the ultimate trust test, let your people score *you!*

Trust Truths

■ We've asked dozens of people from around the globe to tell us how they view trust in the workplace. Here is just some of what we heard.

Trust defined differently.

Human beings are really very much alike . . . and yet, totally unique. So when they talk about trust, people agree that it matters, yet their definitions often vary. What you want and need in order to trust your boss may differ from what someone else wants and needs.

> "That's fascinating that trust, for you, is dependent on building a close connection with your boss. I don't need that at all. In fact, I prefer less, not more, contact. I just need him to do what he promised me he'd do."

Trust as a gift.

Some of your employees will give you trust as a gift. You might not have to prove yourself trustworthy for them to trust you.

> "I'm incredibly trusting . . . sometimes to a fault. I know some people call it being naive, but for me it works most of the time."

Trust must be earned.

Some will say it takes time to develop trust in another. They don't tend to view it as a gift, and they seldom give trust until a person has earned it.

> "It took me a long time to trust my boss completely. That's not because of him. I just have to be convinced someone is worthy before I trust them. He is so honest and has proven to me that he has my back."

Consistency sustains trust.

The more often you repeat trust-building actions, the more apt you are to sustain the trust you've developed with your employees.

> "A mentor suggested I list four to five adjectives that I hoped my employees would all use in describing me. Two of those words were *authentic* and *dependable*. Then my mentor asked what that would look like on a day-to-day basis. I'm very conscious of being the real me in my interactions and of consistently delivering on my promises. My employees have actually told me they trust me."

You can regain trust . . . or can you?

As Grandma used to say, "You can't put the toothpaste back in the tube." But isn't it worth a try? When trust is broken, for whatever reason, some say you can never repair it. No doubt this depends on the situation and the people involved, but we've seen wounds healed and trust rebuilt over time and with a big dose of genuine, heartfelt effort.

> "I had a boss who divulged confidences—mine and others.' I finally told him how much that bothered me and how it

had dented my trust in him. He felt terrible, apologized, and said that would never happen again. It's taken some time, but I've regained the trust I once had in him. And I respect how he handled my feedback and committed to a change."

Trust Dividends

■ What's the return on investment for your trust-building efforts? As your score increases so does:

▶ employee engagement and retention,

▶ customer satisfaction, and

▶ productivity and profitability.

Trust matters. You build it over time with steady action and by doing what you say you'll do.

Get to know your talented people better. Take your authentic self (the real you) to the day-to-day conversations you have with them. If you don't have day-to-day conversations, decide to change that. Go first when they need your guidance. Show support, especially in tough situations, and be their most ardent cheerleader as they take on new risks.

When you ask your talented employees "What will keep you here?," you're asking them to trust you. They'll do that when they trust you to listen carefully and to hold their answers with care.

As Wendy Tan, cofounder of Singapore's Flame Centre, puts it, "When there is trust, the floodgates open and employees really appreciate the opportunity to talk about themselves."

The trust you build with your talented people will pave the way for frank, productive conversations. And those conversations will, in turn, build more trust. If you're nodding your head but are bothered about the time stay interviews might take, stay tuned.

CHAPTER SIX

Will You Make the Time?

■ Will you make the time? This is a good question.

We know you can't manufacture time. But you can effectively manage it and make room in your calendar for something that really matters.

Did your dentist ever tell you to just floss the teeth you hope to keep? Along similar lines, we're saying, "Just hold stay interviews with the *people* you hope to keep." For many of you, that's a lot of people, and it may feel like it will take a lot of time.

MANAGER: I don't have time for these stay interviews.

US: How will you have time, then, to recruit, interview, select, orient, and train replacements for the talent you lose?

It doesn't have to take a lot of time. And there is no best time to ask. It depends on you, your organization's culture, your access to employees, and their styles and preferences.

Oh, the Places You'll Go

■ How, when, and where might you hold stay interviews? It depends. Where does your employee live and work? What does she prefer as far as meeting times and places? What have you done before that worked well for you and your employee? Here are examples of some times and places managers have chosen to have these ongoing conversations with their talent.

ASK EARLY ASK OFTEN

At orientation

It's never too early to start! Managers and recruiters alike now often ask their new hires, "What will keep you here?" They dive deeply into the answers, take notes, and collect crucial clues for hanging on to this new talent.

> One large company decided to have all managers conduct stay interviews immediately after bringing in new employees. They were then expected to have similar conversations with their new recruits after thirty, sixty, and ninety days. Senior leaders read the notes from these interviews. The message is clear in this company that stay interviews matter.

At a layoff announcement

What? Yes. Research shows that a *second wave* of departures follows every downsizing. And the problem is, it's your best people—those with lots of choices—who leave in search of greener grass. Don't wait for the second wave; act now.

> One savvy manufacturing company president called every one of his key employees in for a stay interview immediately following the announcement of a companywide lay-off. He told them he would do everything in his power to

keep their jobs safe. He asked them to please stick around during the crazy, uncertain times to come, and he asked what they needed in order to do that. They all stayed.

At the start of each quarter

Some managers schedule regular stay interviews. That way they won't forget to do them! And of course, managers find their own, unique ways of conducting these chats.

> An engineering organization has invented its own "non-touchy-feely" way to ask. Some engineering managers put the question this way: "I'm gathering data on what it would take to maintain your longevity over time. Can you provide some data points that are important to you, and their projected financial requirements?" The engineering managers then built spreadsheets listing the requirements of each of their direct reports, computed the overall cost, and submitted them for approval through their own chain of command. Approximately 75 percent of each spread-sheet submitted was approved.

At monthly one-on-ones

When stay interviews happen often, they typically take less time. The ongoing dialogue, without large time gaps between chats, creates better understanding and a stronger relationship between employees and managers.

> Leaders of a large financial organization asked all managers to hold stay interviews with the people on their teams. They recommended twenty minutes and suggested that these interviews become part of the regular monthly one-on-ones.

At development discussions

Many managers prefer to separate stay interviews from development conversations. Some separate stay interviews from almost any other conversation. But not always.

> Managers in one organization separate the performance discussion from the development discussion. In contrast, they find that the chat about desires for growth and learning (during the development discussion) provides the perfect context for stay interview questions.

At coffee, at lunch, or on a long walk

We'd choose the walk. But that's just us. What would your employees prefer?

> One manager takes each of his employees out to coffee or lunch at least two times a year—for the express purpose of getting to know them and having them know him a little better. He goes to those meetings with a few of his favorite stay interview questions in mind.

At the resignation meeting

Granted, this is not ideal. Typically, when an employee has a foot out the door, it's simply too late to pull them back in. But if you can't imagine losing them, it's worth a try.

> One manager actually pulled an employee back from the ledge by asking "What would keep you here?" She had accepted another job rather than asking for a promotion. When she told him that, the manager said he couldn't imagine losing her, and he admitted that he had not told her that often enough, nor had he asked what she wanted.

She agreed to stay for a while and to work on a development plan that could position her for the promotion she wanted.

At the perfect time

Stay interviews sometimes happen spontaneously, when the timing is just right. Ultimately, every conversation with your talented employee can have elements (and the impact) of a formal stay interview.

> He had learned how to conduct stay interviews, and it was now a habit. He often scheduled these conversations with his employees, but today it just happened. His employee dropped by the office to say good night and they began chatting about work and life. It felt like the perfect time to tell the employee how much he meant to the team and to ask how he was doing and what would keep him there, hopefully for a long time.

At the office (virtually)

Some of you manage remote teams, with employees spread across the globe. To get work done, you need to somehow stay close to these talented people who are physically far away.

> A manager in a global company said that although face-to-face meetings might be ideal, he and his team can do good work by phone, Skype, or other popular communication platforms. They are now used to it. He conducts regular stay interviews with the talented people he manages from afar. He said those conversations are crucial for engaging the talent on his team, no matter where they live and work.

Interviews That Didn't Work Out As Well

■ Managers and employees alike have sent us stories about stay interviews that didn't work out as well.

> ► *"My boss asked me in the hallway what I wanted to do next in my career. I thought she was firing me."*

> ► *"I learned it's not a great e-mail conversation. I'll try face-to-face or Skype next time."*

> ► *"My boss had several beers before asking me what would keep me on his team. When I started to answer, he nodded off."*

> ► *"I gave an employee a really rough performance review, then asked what her hopes and dreams were. Not a good fit."*

> ► *"My boss started by saying that his boss told him to do this. Hmm."*

> ► *"The men's room was a no-go."*

The More the Merrier

■ Frequent stay interviews will be the new normal—and they are crucial. One manager said, "This is not a 'one and done' kind of thing." You open an ongoing dialogue when you hold a great stay interview. You are making a commitment to your talented people that you'll be asking often and that you hope they'll continue to tell you what they want more of or less of on the job. You hope, too, that they'll come tell you when they want something, if you forget to ask.

Get creative about the how, the when, and the where. And make the time to hold these chats with the people you cannot afford to lose. By the way, one way to save time is to heed the cues that all is not well. Read on. We'll name some of those cues in the next chapter.

HAVE *you* NOTICED LATELY?

CHAPTER SEVEN

Have You Noticed Lately?

■ Have you noticed lately? Noticed what?

Conduct ongoing stay interviews with *everyone* you hope to keep engaged and on your team. Make these conversations a normal part of doing business and of being an effective leader. Take note of those who appear engaged and happy with you and with their jobs. Also take note of those whose job EKG has gone flat for some reason. Could they be considering leaving?

Think about the last talented person who left your team. Did you see it coming? One manager told the following story:

> She walked into my office with a letter in her hand and a stressed look on her face. She said she had just accepted a new job, outside of our company. I was shocked. She was a key employee and had been working on a special project with a cross-functional team of carefully selected people. When I asked why she was leaving, she said that there didn't appear to be a terrific next step for her in our company and this project was winding down. No one, including me, had talked to her about her career path and opportunities for her inside our company. She was unhappy at work and I didn't know it.

Often managers don't know that a key player is about to leave. But actually there are clues, if you know where to look for them. Those clues reside in the signs and symptoms of disengagement and in the workplace situations that predictably drive talent out the door. First, let's look at some of the situations that can cause people to leave your organization.

Put Yourself on Notice

■ Think about your talent. Who might be less than thrilled by one or more of these situations?

Project winding down; no clear next step

The woman highlighted in the story above loved the project she was involved with and began to dread the ending of that great adventure with wonderful, bright colleagues. No one (from inside the organization) was talking to her about an exciting next step.

> **TAKE NOTE:** Are your coveted employees working on projects that are winding down? Have you had conversations with them about what's next?

Blocked promotional or learning opportunities

You've heard about the glass ceiling, which refers to barriers that women face in the workplace. But have you heard about the gray ceiling? That's about the jobs that younger generations want but that baby boomers continue to hang on to, even after traditional retirement age.

> **TAKE NOTE:** Who might feel blocked by the gray ceiling, budget cuts, or company policy? Have you chatted with these folks about possible work-arounds?

Doing the same thing for years, and bored

Some people love doing the same thing for years. Others yearn for something new. It's crucial that you know which is true for the talented people you hope to keep for a while longer.

TAKE NOTE: Which employees have been doing a fairly similar kind of work for a long time? Have you chatted with them about their continued levels of interest?

Perceived or real takeaways

If you've taken away anything—whether it's pay, perks, benefits, a parking space, or even coffee—you could be at risk. People simply don't like takeaways. One group of employees nearly revolted when the CEO announced that the company-provided coffee (a metaphor for generosity) would be removed from the break rooms as a cost-cutting measure. A takeaway might seem like no big deal to you, but it could cause your treasured talent to disengage. They might even seek a company with coffee in the break rooms.

TAKE NOTE: Who is upset about which takeaways? Have you asked more about that, or shown empathy for their loss? Have you helped them learn about the takeaways that seem real but (fortunately) are not?

Poor or no relationship with the boss

Research confirms that people don't leave companies; they leave managers. That's a generalization, and there are exceptions to this rule, but consider what kind of relationship you have with each of your talented employees. Think about how you might improve those crucial connections.

TAKE NOTE: Do you know how good (or not) your relationships are with your talent? Have you asked them what would make the relationship even stronger?

Recent or pending downsizing

Perhaps a layoff happened recently, or maybe the word is out, whether senior leadership intended it or not. People know there will be layoffs and they know they'll be affected. They might lose their jobs, or they might be required to do the work of two colleagues who did leave. Neither is an attractive scenario.

TAKE NOTE: Is a shift happening in your organization? Have you asked the people you can't afford to lose to hang in there through the tough time? Have you reminded them of how much you need them?

Friends have left the company

Research shows that having friends at work correlates positively to employee engagement, productivity, and retention. People love to work with people they like. When great people leave, their friends begin to look around, too.

TAKE NOTE: Have you acknowledged the feelings of those left behind? Did you remember to ask them to stay, even though their friends have gone? Have you found opportunities for them to work with others on projects or assignments, to build new relationships?

No apparent career path

You might think that career paths are a thing of the past, or that the term "career path" is outdated. Perhaps the clearly defined path is no more. Your talented people, however, expect to see clearly outlined opportunities to learn, to grow, to earn more, to achieve, to gain recognition, to build their résumés. When none of that looks possible, they are apt to leave you.

> **TAKE NOTE:** How long has it been since you talked with your employees about their career goals? And have you helped expand their thinking to include learning opportunities and ways to strengthen their skills?

Hot job market

A hot job market always predicts another talent war and the accompanying résumé tsunami! All of a sudden the economy's lights are back on and your best people have more job choices.

> **TAKE NOTE:** Have you openly discussed an improving job market? Are you hoping your employees won't notice? Have you acknowledged the change and told them (again) how important they are to you and to the team?

Watch for Signs and Signals

■ You've identified a few people who might consider leaving because of the situations listed above. Of course, you'll only really know by asking—by holding stay interviews with all of them.

Next, what about the *signs* that someone might be thinking of leaving? Countless managers have told us they could tell, way before employees gave notice, that the employees were going. We asked how the managers could tell—what was different, and what were the signs? Here is some of what we heard:

> ▶ *"She used to contribute in meetings and is now very quiet. Her heart just doesn't seem in it."*

▶ *"Every day now he arrives late, leaves early, and takes l-o-o-ong lunches."*

▶ *"A sign they might leave is when they've made a major update to their LinkedIn profile. Every time I've seen that, it turned out they were looking."*

▶ *"When they stop volunteering for task forces or special projects, I worry that the thrill is gone."*

▶ *"When the former optimist turns pessimistic, I wonder what's up. It could be something else—or it could be the job."*

▶ *"One guy started showing his buddies the job openings he was finding on the Internet. The word got out."*

▶ *"A younger employee asked several people at work to review her updated résumé."*

▶ *"When they used to always join in the Friday night office happy hour and now they don't."*

Which of these signs have you seen? Of course, before you jump to conclusions, you'll want to have conversations with your employees about what you're noticing.

Are Your Antennae Raised?

■ What's going on in your organization or on your team? Are your antennae raised, constantly tuned for situations or signs that someone you cannot afford to lose may be vulnerable to talent theft or is considering leaving?

Try this:

- ▶ **Stop:** Think of each of your direct reports by name.
- ▶ **Look:** Observe them over the coming week. What do you notice? What's new in how they show up, or in how they behave?
- ▶ **Listen:** Really hear what they're saying—to you, to their colleagues, to the customer.

Then ask. Ask about situations that could cause your employee to consider leaving. And ask about signs that suggest they aren't thrilled with work or their workplace—or you! For some, the stay interview comes easily. Others need a few dry runs. Consider this: you couldn't ride a bike on your first try; you needed some practice. Keep reading for some stay interview practice tips.

DOES *practice* MAKE *perfect?*

CHAPTER EIGHT

Does Practice Make Perfect?

■ Does practice make perfect? It gets you closer.

We've asked dozens of managers how *they* get ready for stay interviews. What follows are a few of their answers. Which approaches do you already use? Which new ones might work for you?

Hunching Is Allowed

■ Wait, isn't *hunch* a noun? Yes. And today it's also a new verb: an action you take as you prepare for the stay interview.

One manager hunched, "She's brilliant. In fact, she's one of the best nurses we've ever hired. I can't imagine losing her—and I have no idea if we're vulnerable or not. I pondered that question, along with several others. Is she happy here? Is there something missing? Is she ready for a new challenge? My hunch is that she might want to learn something new, or she could be ready for a bigger job."

That's all there is to it. It's guessing, but it's guessing based on paying attention to what you know and what you've seen and heard. It's not magic and it's not just an intuitive sense, although intuition certainly might play a part.

Hunching helps you to prepare for possibilities and to be ready for some of the challenging requests you might receive when you ask "What will keep you here?"

Open the Door

■ One sales manager we talked to said he was never sure how to open the conversation. So, just as he does during an important meeting with a customer, he decided to start with "Thank you for meeting with me today," and then move to an opening line he has prepared.

Here are some sentence starters you might use for stay interviews. Pick the one that's the honest truth.

▶ *"I hope you know how important you are to me and to this team . . ."*

▶ *"I may not tell you often enough, but you are a key player on my team . . ."*

▶ *"I'm so glad you've joined the team. I look forward to getting to know you better . . ."*

▶ *"Things have been a little crazy around here lately . . ."*

▶ *"As you know, we're facing a layoff. I just want you to know you will not be affected. I need you here . . ."*

▶ *"You have been so amazing these past few months . . ."*

- ► *"I've had four people tell me how well you led our recent project . . ."*

- ► *"From our past conversations, it would appear you are interested in . . ."*

- ► *"The last time we talked you mentioned you wish you knew more about . . ."*

- ► *"This is the first of many chats like this I hope to have with you over the coming months and years . . ."*

- ► *"You've been my right hand . . ."*

- ► *"Yes, I read a book about having chats like this one. I need to know more about what you really want from your work . . ."*

Opening lines should be customized to every person, keeping his or her style, situation, and communication preferences in mind.

Another way to open the door is to extend an invitation. There are many ways to invite someone to have this crucial conversation. One finance manager said he thinks it's important to make it formal. He sent this e-mail to give a key person some time to think and to prepare for the conversation:

Hi, Sara. I look forward to our chat over coffee next week. As I mentioned, I'd like for us to talk about your strengths, interests, and values and how we are, or are not, fully utilizing these in your current role. Over the coming weeks I would like to explore what is working really well and giving you high satisfaction and how we can enhance this over the coming months. You are key to our success and we hope to keep you here for a long time.

Try a Test Run

■ For how long have you been conducting stay interviews? Years? Months? Minutes? Depending on your answer, you might decide that a little or a *lot* of practice is in order. After all, these chats could influence the stay-or-go decisions of your best people.

  Here are some unique ways to practice. Some of these methods take minutes; others take more time.

Test run 1: Bev's approach

Bev's favorite approach is to do this herself. She asks herself the questions she plans to ask her talented employees. Then she notices her reactions. Which questions really get her thinking, or seem too intrusive, or help her to go deeper? She says, "This is a great way for me to select my favorite questions for upcoming stay interviews." Bev's favorite questions to herself include:

  ▸ Why do I stay?

  ▸ What keeps me going?

  ▸ What do I want to learn more about?

  ▸ What about my job gives me the most thrills? When was the last time I got to do that?

  ▸ Who do I enjoy collaborating with? How can I do more of that?

Test run 2: Sharon's approach

Sharon suggests that the manager find a practice buddy at work or at home (or at the pub). The practice buddy plays the role of the treasured employee. The manager starts by thinking of this employee she hopes to keep. She then jots down her hunches about what that person might want and shares those hunches with her practice buddy. Finally, she creates her opening lines.

Then they talk! The practice buddy pretends this is real and pushes fairly hard for the things she really wants.

They debrief by asking "What did the manager do best in the stay interview?" and "What could she improve on?" The manager takes notes as she gets the feedback.

Test run 3: A peer practice approach

As part of a two-day leadership summit, one company president decided to introduce the concept of stay interviews as a crucial component of a companywide engagement/retention initiative. Here is a brief overview of his stay interview clinic with one hundred twenty leaders.

- ▶ **Introduction to stay interviews.** We discussed why it's important to hold these conversations, why it's hard, and why we avoid it. We presented the four steps to handle tough requests, including examples.

- ▶ **Role-play activity.** We formed three-person groups, including a leader, an employee, and an observer/scribe. They conducted stay interviews three times, trading places so that everyone played each role. Then we debriefed the exercise with the whole group.

- ▶ **Action plan for implementing stay interviews companywide.** We crafted a plan that included such things as working within division teams, forming expectations for all, timeline creation, development of an interview form, creation of follow-up protocol, and monitoring and reporting.

Test run 4: A learn-as-you-go approach

Just do it. One manager said he didn't want to practice with a buddy or convene a clinic. He said he subscribed to the learn-as-you-go method of practice. He suggested a few guidelines that increased the odds of success for him and that might help others:

- ▶ **Start with a favorite employee.** Yes, we do have them, and chances are, that person likes (and trusts) you too. That relationship creates a positive context for almost any conversation you want to have, including the stay interview.

- ▶ **Consider carefully the *where* and the *when* for your stay interview.** Especially as you're learning, you'll want a relaxed environment and time frame.

- ▶ **Do your homework and prepare.** Don't wing it. Stay interviews are crucial conversations and work best when you're focused and prepared.

- ▶ **Seek feedback.** Have the conversation, and then ask this treasured employee, "How did that work for you? What could I have done differently to make it an even better stay interview?"

Questions, Questions, More Questions

■ Some of you will find it easier to practice if you have more questions from which to choose. Here are some of our favorites, drawn from our sixteen years of research on the question "What keeps people?" We've learned that managers hold the keys to engagement and retention. We've also learned that successful managers do three things very well. They:

- ▶ support employee development and growth;

- ▶ have a management style that breeds loyalty; and

- ▶ create a work environment that people love.

Consider including some of these questions in your stay interview preparation.

Support employee development and growth

The belief that everyone wants a promotion is a myth. Our own research suggests that people want to grow, learn, be challenged, and become more employable. Find out what people want from you and from their organization by asking:

- ▶ *"Which of your team skills do your colleagues value the most? How do you know? Based on their feedback, which skills do you hope to improve?"*

- ▶ *"What would you like to be doing in the next two to three years?"*

- ▶ *"What is the most enriching aspect of your work?"*

- ▶ *"Are you getting the mentoring you want and need from me? From others?"*

- ▶ *"What opportunities do you see or might you want to explore in our organization?"*

- ▶ *"How many different goals or pathways do you see for yourself here?"*

- ▶ *"What could I do to help you connect to others in the organization?"*

Have a management style that breeds loyalty

Loyalty is not dead. It may have changed shape over the years, but it is still alive. Your management style has a lot to do with your employees' levels of commitment to you and to your organization. So how is your style working? Use questions like these to find out:

- ▸ *"How do you like to be recognized? Rewarded?"*

- ▸ *"What kind of support or direction do you need from me? What aren't you getting?"*

- ▸ *"In which areas do you wish I would give you more feedback? Praise?"*

- ▸ *"How can I help you feel more accomplished and successful at work?"*

- ▸ *"Does the job measure up to what I promised when we first met? Where are we on or off? How might we course-correct?"*

- ▸ *"How are we similar? How are we different? How might our differences get in the way?"*

- ▸ *"You'd be thrilled if I changed what about myself? About the job?"*

Create a work environment that people love

There's a well-known quote (attributed to Peter Drucker) that "culture eats strategy for breakfast." The concept brings a nod or a smile to most people. Company cultures can cause a match or a mismatch between individuals and their organizations. And although you as a manager can't dictate a company's culture, you can greatly influence your own department's culture and help your employees get more of what they want from their workplace. Try asking these questions to learn more:

► *"How does the work pace and schedule work for you? How does it work against you? Is there anything we need to adjust?"*

► *"What have you learned about what counts in this organization?"*

► *"What most surprised you about our culture?"*

► *"What was the most difficult culture shift for you to make?"*

► *"What do you know now that you wish you had known earlier?"*

► *"How does our work environment support fun, health, and family? How could we do better in those areas?"*

► *"How can I help you get more of what you want, given the culture of our company?"*

Yes, Practice Does Make Perfect

■ Someone said to us, "Stay interviews start easy and get easier."
Well said. The more stay interviews you conduct, the easier
they become—for you and for your employees. You will quickly
learn to use these conversations regularly and as part of normal
dialogue with your talented people. You'll discover your favorite opening lines, your favorite places to hold these chats, and
of course, your own, unique favorite questions. Want some real
stories? Check out the next chapter.

HOW'S *that* WORKING FOR *you?*

HELP THEM
SAY
WHY THEY
STAY

CHAPTER NINE

How's That Working for You?

■ How's that working for you? We've asked hundreds of managers that question over the past sixteen years. Many respond, "I've learned a lot . . . and used what I learned."

Stay Interviews That Worked

■ Here are three success stories. Read each one, then answer this question: What did the boss do well in this stay interview? At the end of the chapter, check out our opinion about what these managers did well.

Pulling him back from the ledge

MANAGER: Thanks for meeting with me today. I know that times are tense right now. Ever since the layoff announcement, I've been concerned about you. I hope you know that I want you to stay.

YOUNG ENGINEER: Well, to be honest, I've updated my résumé and have gone on a couple of interviews. I think I'll have a job offer by the end of the week. I know the younger engineers are the first ones to go during a reduction in force. I'm one of those people.

MANAGER: You have a great future here, and I'll do everything I can to protect you during these downsizings. I need you here!

YOUNG ENGINEER: Thanks so much. I love my job here. It just seemed a matter of time before I was let go, so I thought I'd better look out for myself. It feels great to think you're looking out for me too.

What happened? He stayed. He learned, he took on senior roles, and he contributed in major ways to the organization's success.

She wants your job

MANAGER: Thanks so much for taking time to chat today. I'd like to talk about what will keep you engaged and on my team—for a long time to come! What will keep you here?

ADVERTISING DIRECTOR: I've been thinking about what I'd say, ever since you invited me to have this chat about my future here. Frankly, I want your job.

MANAGER: Hopefully you don't want it tomorrow. [Laughs.] Well, let's start working on that. Have you thought about what you'd need to do to prepare for that step?

ADVERTISING DIRECTOR: I'm sure there are things I need to learn, but I don't know exactly what they are or how to learn them.

MANAGER: Let's craft a plan together. I'll think about things I believe you would need to learn or develop, given your goal to have my job. You do the same. We can meet next Friday to compare notes and begin to create a development road map. Does that make sense?

ADVERTISING DIRECTOR: That sounds great. I'm really excited about this. Thanks so much!

What happened? Together, they crafted a plan to get the advertising director started. She attended leadership classes and took on diverse learning assignments. When her boss was promoted a few years later, she got his job.

Keep him—just a little while longer

MANAGER: I'm really sorry to hear you're thinking of retiring. The entire team counts on you for so much. You've got the experience and the customer connections, and you know almost everything there is to know about this company. Is there anything I can say or do to convince you to stay—even if it's for only a little while longer?

KEY ACCOUNT SALESMAN: That is so nice of you to say. It makes me feel great. To be honest, I think the time is right for me to go. I don't really see anything new or very exciting for me in this company.

MANAGER: What if together we could find something new or exciting?

KEY ACCOUNT SALESMAN: Like what?

MANAGER: Well, I've noticed how you work with the young salespeople as they come on board. I think you're a natural mentor. What if we created a more formal mentoring role for you? I think it would be a win–win.

KEY ACCOUNT SALESMAN: Hmm. That does sound intriguing. Let's talk more about that.

What happened? The account salesman stayed for another two years. He mentored several new hires, speeding up their learning and helping to establish their connections with key customers. The new hires loved him and he loved them. He felt very rewarded by the new relationships he formed and the help that he gave to the next generation of sales professionals.

What Went Well?

■ Here's our take on what each boss did well.

First manager: She was proactive and courageous. She identified the elephant in the room—that downsizing could cause people to undertake a job search and even leave. She did not react negatively when the young engineer told her he had been interviewing. She asked him to stay and said she'd try her best to protect him from layoffs. She was clear about how important he was to her.

Second manager: He held a stay interview, knowing full well that the advertising director would want something big! Little did he know it was his job. But he handled her response with a cool demeanor and a bit of humor. He laid out a plan for them to work on together and didn't feel pressured to offer anything on the spot. He made it clear that this would be a process and that the advertising director had room to develop before she could take on his job.

Third manager: Like the first two, this manager took the first step and asked his employee about the rumor that the employee might retire. The manager clearly stated why this treasured person was so valuable to him and to the organization and then asked him to stay—at least a little while longer. He listened well when his employee said the words *new* and *exciting,* and he echoed those words right back, in search of something the account salesman might be interested in.

Action ... the Key to Success

■ You've conducted great stay interviews with your wonderful employees. You're done, right? Not really. In fact, you've just started. Now it's time to *do* something, based on what you've learned. The actions you take depend on the requests you heard. You might do one or more of the following:

- ► Seek information about the request.

- ► Do what you promised to do.

- ► Ask how it's going.

- ► Record your learning.

- ► Discover what else they need from you.

- ► Set up the next chat.

It seems pretty intuitive, but it's worth stating directly: be ready to take action when you conduct stay interviews with the people you hope will stay and play on your team.

What about the Naysayers?

■ We would be less than honest if we didn't include input from some managers who haven't (yet) embraced stay interviews. Here are a few of the most common push-backs—and our thoughts about them.

> **MANAGER:** What's in it for me to take the time and effort to do stay interviews?

> **US:** What's in it for you? You'll have employees who no longer wonder whether you value them, who appreciate being asked what they really want, who bring more of their discretionary effort to work, and who will stay—at least a little while longer.

> **MANAGER:** My boss has never done this with me. Why should I do it with my employees?

> **US:** It's sad about your boss. Maybe he never thought of it or learned how to do it. Leave a copy of this book on his desk.

> **MANAGER:** Isn't this pandering to employees?

> **US:** It could be viewed that way. Or it could be viewed as strategic management.

> **MANAGER:** The timing is off. We just announced a downsizing.

US: The timing is on. Conduct stay interviews with anyone you hope will stay (despite the uncertainty). These people will help you stay on track after the dust settles.

MANAGER: My heart's not in this. Should I try to do it anyway?

US: It is crucial that the stay interview be authentic, that you honestly mean every word you're saying to this talented employee. If your heart's not in it, figure out why that is. Adapt the timing, the process, or the script so that it works for you—then give it another go.

High Note

■ We believe in ending on a high note. So here are six more illustrations of how stay interviews made a positive difference—and in some cases saved the day.

► *"A twenty-three-year veteran of our company had his résumé updated and ready to distribute. The stay interview, along with my follow-through on his requests, saved this key employee for my team and the organization."*

► *"I learned that an employee was dissatisfied and ready to leave. He was unhappy with the job location. During the stay interview, I was able to negotiate a two-year commitment from him in exchange for my agreement to help him transfer to his preferred destination."*

► *"I learned that one employee really valued information, being kept in the loop, and being asked for input. I was very glad to know this and made a commitment to this talented employee to offer those things more readily, going forward."*

▶ *"I assigned the IT [information technology] component of one employee's job to another employee, after discovering in stay interviews with both that one disliked IT and the other wanted more of an IT role."*

▶ *"I noticed that one quality employee seemed stressed and was not performing well. During the stay interview she stated that she was not interested in a promotion. I moved her primary role to a lower-profile, less-stressful desk job. She was thrilled and is now performing very well."*

▶ *"A seven-year employee felt neglected. The stay interview uncovered her interests, and I rewired her job to give her more of what she wanted. I realized that, quite unintentionally, she was being overlooked and taken for granted. Now that she is doing more of what she loves, my perspective has completely changed, and I now see her skills as a huge asset to our team."*

What if these managers hadn't asked?

The Bottom Line

■ Stay interviews are not the only way to engage and retain talent, but they are foundational to that goal. Without them, you're left wondering what your talented people really want. Stop wondering and start asking.

STAY INTERVIEWS
→ PREVENT ←
EXIT INTERVIEWS

Parting Note

YOU HOPE YOUR talented people will stay—at least for a while longer. Good people always have choices, and your competition wants them. There are so many things you can do to keep them engaged and on your team. But how do you really know what will work with each individual? We hope this playbook helps you answer that question.

Stop guessing and start asking. Ask early and ask often. Every conversation is an opportunity to learn and to further engage your talent.

The stay interview is just a very conscious way of exploring what matters most and then partnering with your employees to make it happen.

The Spillover Effect

■ Have you heard of the spillover effect? It happens when a seemingly small or insignificant thing spills over and affects many others. Ever notice, for instance, how laughter gets other people laughing?

Stay interviews have a positive spillover effect. Pass this playbook to the managers who report to you. Encourage them to hold stay interviews with their direct reports. The process catches on and can spread increased happiness, effectiveness, productivity, and employee retention. Many organizations are counting on this spillover effect and are asking all managers at all levels to hold these important conversations.

Try This

- ▸ Ask each employee what will keep him or her in your company or on your team.

- ▸ Make a note of every employee's answer.

- ▸ Every month, review the notes and ask yourself what you've done for that person that relates to his or her requests.

- ▸ Have another chat. Stay interviews are not a one-time thing. They need to be authentic and they need to be ongoing.

Let us know how it goes!

Bev and Sharon

Acknowledgments

■ When we joined together to write the first edition of *Love 'Em or Lose 'Em* in 1999, we didn't think we would be writing acknowledgments more than once. What a happy surprise for us. We've had the wonderful opportunity to write them five times for *Love 'Em or Lose 'Em* (always new people to thank) and once for *Love It, Don't Leave It*. Now we have a chance to write some thank yous to the individuals who helped with this (daughter of *Love 'Em*) book.

Our first thank you goes to the Berrett-Koehler team and to our editor, Steve Piersanti, president of Berrett-Koehler. Although we know it is not good karma to say "never," we both believe that we would never take our work to anyone else. Steve has always been our biggest cheerleader, wise critic, and supportive taskmaster. He makes us feel wonderful. Yes, even when he says (as he did with this book), "You are only 70 percent there." We thought we were done, but once again, he was right. Thank you, Steve, for all you do to help us craft a better book.

Our second thank you goes to our voice editor, Nancy Breuer. Nancy worked on every edition of *Love 'Em*, as well as its sister, *Love It, Don't Leave It*. We would not think of passing our work on to our publisher without Nancy's magic touch. She is meticulous in her art, honest in her critique, and generous in her praise.

Our artist, Mike Rhode, and Berrett-Koehler's artistic director, Dianne Platner, had the most amazing patience and never (at least not that we saw) lost their tempers or their willingness to have another go at the design elements. This team stuck with our vision for the book and with us. And for that, we are grateful. Thanks also to our dynamic production team, with Berrett-Koehler's Lasell Whipple and Seventeenth Street Studios' Naomi Schiff at the helm. You helped bring this work alive.

Lorianne Speaks, Bev's executive assistant, said she wanted "in" from the very beginning. She reviewed, she commented, she interpreted Bev's hieroglyphics, and she brought a crucial, fresh perspective to the party. Thanks to her, we stayed on task and connected to one another all the way through.

We were lucky in that we had a large number of facilitators in client organizations who had taught the concepts of the stay interview as described in our workshops and keynotes. They told us what more was needed, gave us real examples and suggestions, and encouraged us to include their ideas. The Career Systems team has been teaching the stay interview concepts for more than fifteen years. They were able to reach thousands of managers around the globe, and they brought us stories and recommendations that we used liberally throughout the book. We owe them all a giant thanks!

We hand selected a brain trust that helped us fine-tune this book. It was made up of friends and family, colleagues and clients, many of whom actually read every single word, often more than once. They told us the truth; a few even suggested we start over—in a loving way, of course. Our heartfelt thanks goes to Ann Jordan, Mike Evans, Ann Ratcliff, Donna Kohlbacker, Beverly Crowell, Diana Koch, Andrew Jones, Shelby Earl, Bette Krakau, Wendy

Tan, Katie Wacek, Lindy Williams, Evaan Portillo, Alan McIver, Andrew Buckingham, Joel Tobin, Halelly Azulay, and Lucy Lei.

We sincerely appreciate our husbands, Barry and Mike. They've been through the book-writing adventure several times now and they supported us wholeheartedly in doing it again. Sharon thanks Mike for "bringing his leadership perspective, loving patience, and great dinners to the party!" Bev thanks Barry for "always being in my corner, no matter what the project is." We want them both to stay.

Finally, we appreciate and thank each other. We have different skill sets, different backgrounds, different work experience, and different organizations. Those differences make our work together interesting, sometimes even challenging, and always productive. We know that what we create together is far better than what we could do alone.

Index

Skill Building
Beyond the Book

■ Career Systems International and the Jordan Evans Group have developed an array of learning solutions designed to support organizations around the globe. Our learning solutions come in all shapes and sizes. They are instructor-led and either face-to-face or virtual. We deliver in all modalities and all durations. Micro-learning, e-learning, assessment tools, portals, and insight tools are available. Training of internal trainers or line managers is a popular delivery vehicle, and our experienced facilitators are located around the globe.

After reading *Hello Stay Interviews, Goodbye Talent Loss,* many managers will need a chance to practice the new approaches they've learned. Our learning solutions offer templates, techniques, and tools that can be immediately implemented. It sets up the stay interview as an ongoing conversation that is varied and repeatable.

The stay interview is only one of a number of practical approaches to engaging and retaining talent. Another offering, based on the best seller *Love 'Em or Lose 'Em,* provides a full array of engagement strategies that can be matched to the individual needs of each employee and organization. This learning solution helps managers understand their role and instill the confidence in holding conversations as they develop much-needed critical skills.

Engagement is not the manager's job alone. Employees are responsible for their own work-life satisfaction. This point is made

in *Love It, Don't Leave It,* and this learning solution empowers employees to take ownership of this role. It provides straight-talking advice and strategies that match the learning solution designed for their managers. It's a partnership, after all.

Career development is one of the major drivers of engagement

and retention. **CareerPower** and **CareerPower for Coaches** are designed to help employees take charge of their own development and build the partnership with their managers. *Help Them Grow or Watch Them Go* is another approach that helps leaders hold real-time, real-world, relevant career conversations in a time-starved, pressure cooker world.

For some, the best way to maintain the skills required to engage, retain, and develop is to be involved with a one-on-one or group coaching experience. Our **solution-based coaching model** focuses on creating and sustaining critical coaching conversations that further ignite the vital connections between employees, their managers, and the organization as a whole. It provides an opportunity to build, practice, and polish these critical skills.

There are no magic bullets or one-size-fits-all solutions. Our

consulting services help organizations define, address, develop, deliver, and assess unique organizational needs. Organizations with a talent mind-set provide the knowledge and tools that employees and managers need to remain competitive. Success demands that learning solutions be integrated with other human resource systems and designed for each unique culture.

The authors and senior consultants are frequent **keynote presenters** at associations, organizations, and other mission-critical events. They have long track records and are able to kick off initiatives for any engagement, retention, or development event where inspiring an audience and mobilizing action is imperative.

Since 1998, the authors and their organizations have been conducting research  to understand "stay factors" in organizations. They publish frequent white papers called **"What Keeps You?"** Their research cuts across geography, organizations, industries, age, and other demographic factors. Their findings offer insight into what keeps today's worker in and committed to an organization. This research is continually updated and can be found on the Career Systems International website.

About the Authors

■ The authors of this book began their journey together in 1997, when they conducted research for the first edition of *Love 'Em or Lose 'Em*. They were passionate about providing managers with practical tools and strategies for engaging, developing, and retaining the talent on their teams. They still are.

Beverly Kaye founded Career Systems International (CSI) more than thirty years ago, and it has become a global leader in developing and delivering innovative, action-based talent management solutions. With an emphasis on engagement and retention, as well as its flagship offerings in career development, Career Systems International supports organizations globally.

Bev was honored with the Distinguished Contribution award from the Association for Talent Development for her groundbreaking and continual contributions to workplace learning. Her first book, *Up Is Not the Only Way*, continues to be a classic in the career development field. Her recent book, coauthored with Julie Winkle Giulioni, *Help Them Grow or Watch Them Go*, maintains that status. She earned her doctorate at UCLA.

Bev is a transplanted Jersey girl who has made her home in Los Angeles with her husband, Barry; her daughter, Lindsey; and her dog, Roxy. She is a frequent keynote speaker. Visit her website, **www.CareerSystemsIntl.com**, or e-mail her at **HQ@CareerSystemsIntl.com**.

Sharon Jordan-Evans, president of the Jordan Evans Group, is a pioneer in the field of employee engagement and retention. She works with the people companies can least afford to lose—their high-performers. Sharon is a sought-after keynote speaker for Fortune 500 companies such as American Express, Boeing, Disney, Lockheed, Microsoft, Monster, and Universal Studios. She has a master's degree in organization development and is a certified executive coach.

Sharon also serves as a resource for a number of national media, including National Public Radio (NPR), *Business 2.0, Chief Executive, CIO, Harvard Management Update, Working Woman, Investor's Business Daily, Business Week,* and the *Los Angeles Times.*

Sharon was born in the Northwest and now lives in Cambria, California, with her husband, Mike, and a very smart shih tzu named Oreo. She has four grown children and five adorable grandchildren.

To learn more about Sharon's work and to view her speaker video, visit her website at **www.jeg.org**. To contact Sharon, please e-mail her at **sharon@jeg.org**.

Author Day at Berrett-Koehler

About the Illustrator

- Mike Rohde, founder of Rohdesign, is an interface and experience designer in Milwaukee, Wisconsin. He creates custom illustrations for companies, agencies, and design firms.

  Mike has illustrated numerous books, including the *New York Times* best sellers *Rework and Remote* by 37signals, *The $100 Startup* by Chris Guillebeau, and *The Little Book of Talent* by Daniel Coyle.

  Mike has written two books on sketchnoting: *The Sketchnote Handbook* and *The Sketchnote Workbook*. He also speaks at events and presents workshops that teach people sketchnoting techniques.

  You can view samples of Mike's work at **www.Rohdesign.com**.

By Beverly Kaye and Sharon Jordan-Evans

Love 'Em or Lose 'Em

Getting Good People to Stay, 5th Edition

Talent is everything. That's why engagement and retention matter more than ever before. Every employee who walks out the door costs the company up to 200 percent of his or her annual salary to replace, and survey after survey reports that employees are unhappy and not working up to their full potential. As a manager, you need your best people to stay with you longer, fully engaged and producing at their peak. The latest edition of this *Wall Street Journal* bestseller offers twenty-six simple strategies—from A to Z—that managers can use to address their employees' real concerns and keep them engaged. Good economy or bad, your best people always have choices. Will they choose you? You have the power to make a difference. *Love 'Em or Lose 'Em* shows you what to do.

Paperback, 328 pages, ISBN 978-1-60994-884-9
PDF ebook, ISBN 978-1-60994-885-6

Berrett–Koehler Publishers, Inc.
www.bkconnection.com

800.929.2929

Berrett–Koehler
Publishers

Berrett-Koehler is an independent publisher dedicated to an ambitious mission: Connecting people and ideas to create a world that works for all.

We believe that the solutions to the world's problems will come from all of us, working at all levels: in our organizations, in our society, and in our own lives. Our BK Business books help people make their organizations more humane, democratic, diverse, and effective (we don't think there's any contradiction there). Our BK Currents books offer pathways to creating a more just, equitable, and sustainable society. Our BK Life books help people create positive change in their lives and align their personal practices with their aspirations for a better world.

All of our books are designed to bring people seeking positive change together around the ideas that empower them to see and shape the world in a new way.

And we strive to practice what we preach. At the core of our approach is Stewardship, a deep sense of responsibility to administer the company for the benefit of all of our stakeholder groups including authors, customers, employees, investors, service providers, and the communities and environment around us. Everything we do is built around this and our other key values of quality, partnership, inclusion, and sustainability.

This is why we are both a B-Corporation and a California Benefit Corporation—a certification and a for-profit legal status that require us to adhere to the highest standards for corporate, social, and environmental performance.

We are grateful to our readers, authors, and other friends of the company who consider themselves to be part of the BK Community. We hope that you, too, will join us in our mission.

A BK Business Book

We hope you enjoy this BK Business book. BK Business books pioneer new leadership and management practices and socially responsible approaches to business. They are designed to provide you with groundbreaking and practical tools to transform your work and organizations while upholding the triple bottom line of people, planet, and profits. High-five!

To find out more, visit **www.bkconnection.com**.

Berrett–Koehler
Publishers

Connecting people and ideas
to create a world that works for all

Dear Reader,

Thank you for picking up this book and joining our worldwide community
of Berrett-Koehler readers. We share ideas that bring positive change into
people's lives, organizations, and society.

To welcome you, we'd like to offer you a free e-book. You can pick from
among twelve of our bestselling books by entering the promotional code
BKP92E here: http://www.bkconnection.com/welcome.

When you claim your free e-book, we'll also send you a copy of our e-news-
letter, the *BK Communiqué*. Although you're free to unsubscribe, there are
many benefits to sticking around. In every issue of our newsletter you'll find

- A free e-book
- Tips from famous authors
- Discounts on spotlight titles
- Hilarious insider publishing news
- A chance to win a prize for answering a riddle

Best of all, our readers tell us, "Your newsletter is the only one I actually
read." So claim your gift today, and please stay in touch!

Sincerely,

Charlotte Ashlock
Steward of the BK Website

Questions? Comments? Contact me at bkcommunity@bkpub.com.

Certified Sourcing
www.sfiprogram.org
SFI-00453

Certified

Corporation
bcorporation.net